## THIS BOOK

This book looks at the Bahá'í Faith from the viewpoint of two Bahá'í children. Here you will read about their beliefs, the history of their religion, and their family and community life. You will discover the answers to the questions: What does it mean to be a Bahá'í and what are the teachings that Bahá'ís follow?

The Bahá'í Faith, which began in Persia (Iran) in the nineteenth century, is found today in almost every country in the world, and together Bahá'ís are working to bring about world unity and a lasting peace.

## ABOUT THE AUTHOR

Patrick Vickers is a Middle School teacher and has been a Bahá'í since he was twenty years old. For the past two years he has served on the Standing Advisory Council for Religious Education (SACRE) in Coventry. He lives in Warwickshire with his wife and daughter and enjoys birdwatching and listening to music in his spare time.

The gardens of Bahjí in the Holy Land

# The Bahá'í Faith

by

Patrick Vickers

ONEWORLD
OXFORD

The Bahá'í Faith

Oneworld Publications
(Sales and Editorial)
185 Banbury Rd, Oxford, OX2 7AR, England

Oneworld Publications
(U.S. Sales Office)
42 Broadway
Rockport, MA 01966, U.S.A.


Second revised edition 1994



A CIP record for this book is available from the British Library

ISBN 1-85168-030-6

Printed and bound in Singapore by Craft Print

Photo Credits: Adam Thorne 7, 8, 9, 11, 16, 19, 25, 26, 34, 36-7, 41; The Bahá'í International Audio-Visual Department 2, 10, 12, 13, 14, 17, 21, 29, 30, 31, 32, 42-3, 44, 45, 46-7, 48-9, 55, 58, 60; Greg Dahl 42, 43; Stuart Davis 21 tr; Alan Duncan 53; Rocky Grove 15; Juliet Mabey 33; Michael Sours 21 br & bl, 27; Ann Vickers 34 b; Rebecca Vickers 28.

Cover photograph shows the Shrine of the Báb on Mount Carmel in Haifa, Israel

*Approved by the*
NATIONAL SPIRITUAL ASSEMBLY
OF THE BAHÁ'ÍS OF THE UNITED KINGDOM

# Contents


**A Bahá'í Family** 7

Serene and Sahar 8
Their Parents 9

**Bahá'í Beliefs** 10

Thinking for Ourselves 11
Humanity is One 12
Together but Different 13
All Countries Working Together 14
A Fairer Way of Life 15
Men and Women are Equal 16
Education for Everybody 17
A World Language 18
Kindness to Animals 19
Religions Should Agree 20
Messengers of God 21
The Soul 24
Life After Death 25
Prayer 26

**The History of the Bahá'í Faith** 28

The Báb 29
Bahá'u'lláh 30
'Abdu'l-Bahá 32

**Community Life** 33

Bahá'í Children's Classes 34
The Bahá'í Calendar 35
The Feast 36
Bahá'í Holy Days 38
Bahá'í Weddings 40

**The Bahá'í World** 41

Who is a Bahá'í? 42
Bahá'í Assemblies 44
Bahá'í Holy Places 45
Bahá'í Houses of Worship 46
Social Projects 48

**Activities** 50
**Topic Work** 52
**Facts and Figures** 54
**Glossary** 56
**Index** 61

A Bahá'í Family

# Serene and Sahar

Serene and Sahar belong to the newest world religion. It is called the Bahá'í Faith and they are Bahá'ís.

# Their Parents

Serene and Sahar live on a farm with their parents and two younger brothers. Their mother and father grow large fields of vegetables, such as sweetcorn and peas. They are also Bahá'ís. Their mother was brought up in a Bahá'í family, and their father became a Bahá'í after hearing about the Bahá'í Faith and making up his own mind.

# Bahá'í Beliefs

Bahá'u'lláh, the founder of the Bahá'í Faith, wanted people to live together in peace. He said, 'The earth is but one country and mankind its citizens'. Bahá'ís believe that if we follow His teachings we will make the world a happier and better place. Here are some of the teachings that Serene and Sahar learn about:

# Thinking for Ourselves

One thing Bahá'í children are taught is to learn to think for themselves and make up their own minds about things. They are encouraged to learn about other faiths and to make friends with children from all religions. Bahá'u'lláh said '. . . see with thine own eyes and not through the eyes of others'.

# Humanity is One

We should love everyone, whether they are black or brown or white, or rich or poor. God has made us all different, so that life is more interesting. Bahá'u'lláh said that the human race is like a garden where all the flowers are different colours. If all the flowers were the same colour, it would not be so beautiful. People are also different colours and together we all make a wonderful garden of people.

## Together but Different

We should try to like and understand people who are different from us, and not be prejudiced about them. Then we can stop fighting and live together in peace and unity. But unity should not mean that we have to give up our different customs and ways of life. It is these differences that make the world such an interesting and special place.

# All Countries Working Together

Instead of fighting, all the countries of the world should help one another to make life better for everyone. This way we can work together to solve the world's problems, like poverty, hunger, disease and pollution. There needs to be a world parliament to co-ordinate this.

# A Fairer Way of Life

The world should have a fairer money system so that there are no very poor countries like there are today. Although there is enough food in the world for everyone to share, millions of people are hungry all the time. This must not be allowed to happen any longer.

# Men and Women are Equal

In many countries men and women are not treated the same. This is not fair. Bahá'ís believe that men and women are like the two wings of a bird. Both wings must be strong for the bird of humanity to fly. Bahá'í boys and girls are brought up to think of each other as equals.

## Education for Everybody

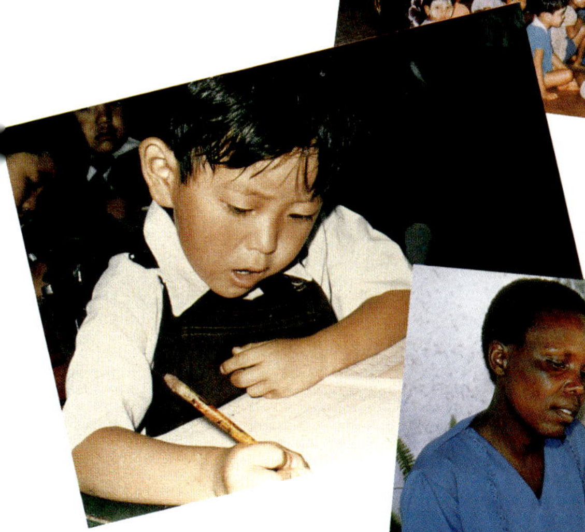

All children in the world should be given the chance to learn. This way everyone can develop all their talents. There are millions of children who do not have a school to go to. At school, we should study what it means to be part of one world.

## A World Language

สันติภาพแห่งโลก

МИРУ-МИР

שלום בעולם

համաշխարհային խաղաղություն

世界
和平

صلح جهانی

WORLD
PEACE

विश्व शान्ति

ΠΑΓΚΟΣΜΙΑ ΕΙΡΗΝΗ

A world language should be chosen. Every school should teach the world language as well as the language of that area. Then all the people in the world will be able to talk to one another.

# Kindness to Animals

Bahá'ís believe we should respect the earth and all God's creatures. We must be kind to every living thing. Animals and birds feel pain like we do, but they cannot complain if people are cruel to them. We should care for them if they are ill, hungry or thirsty.

## Religions Should Agree

In all the religions God has given us special teachings to help us develop ourselves. Each religion asks us to love and help everyone. They all teach that we should treat other people as we would like to be treated ourselves. Bahá'ís believe that people of all religions should respect each other, and pray and work together for peace.

# Messengers of God

Bahá'ís believe that all the Messengers of God brought a special message from God which told the people of the time how God wanted them to live. Some of these Messengers lived a very long time ago, but on the next pages are some of the ones we know about.

## Messengers of God

- **Abraham** Abraham taught that there was one God. He was sent away from His country because of what He taught.

- **Moses** Moses led the Israelites out of Egypt, and gave them laws for their new life. The most famous ones are called the Ten Commandments. His followers are known as Jews, and their history and teachings can be found in the Torah (the Old Testament).

- **Krishna** In the holy books of the Hindus, Krishna teaches us that God appears to mankind in every age. He also taught that we should respect every living thing.

- **Zoroaster** Zoroaster lived in Persia, where the king used Zoroaster's teachings about good and evil to make his empire a better place to live. His followers are called Zoroastrians, and their holy book is called the Avesta.

- **Buddha** The Buddha, the Enlightened One, was an Indian prince who gave up all His possessions to teach the people right living and right thinking. His followers are called Buddhists.

- **Jesus** Jesus taught the message of love and forgiveness, but the leaders of the time did not like what He said and had Him crucified. Those who believe in Him and follow His teachings are called Christians.

- **Muḥammad** Muḥammad told the people of Arabia about God, Jesus and about the laws of Moses. He gave them new laws and teachings for His time, and you can read about them in the book called the Qu'rán (Koran).

- **The Báb** The Báb lived in Persia, and He gave His followers new teachings and told them to prepare for the Promised One, a great teacher who would unite all the peoples of the world.

- **Bahá'u'lláh** Bahá'u'lláh brought new teachings for our time. He taught that we must live together in peace and unity.

There have also been other Messengers in parts of the world that had no writing and they have not left us books. There have also been other great teachers, such as Confucius and Guru Nanak. Bahá'ís believe that we should take notice of every good and wise thing all these teachers have taught.

## The Soul

Bahá'ís believe that the most important part of us is our soul, even though we cannot see it. We need to look after our soul, just as we need to eat in order to grow and have a healthy body. If we pray, and read and think about the Word of God it will help our soul to develop. Good ways of living also help a person's soul to progress and to keep getting closer to God after the person dies. We should try to be:

- *Truthful*
- *Kind*
- *Polite*
- *Obedient*
- *Hard-working*
- *Helpful*
- *Generous*
- *Friendly to everyone*
- *Fair*
- *Honest*
- *Clean*
- *A comfort to people who are ill*

We should never say unkind things about people behind their backs. Instead we should always look at their good points.

# Life After Death

Bahá'ís believe that when we die our soul lives on. It is a bit like the way a baby is born. First it lives in its mother's womb where it does not even know the outside world exists. When it is born, it finds a whole new world which is even more wonderful than the warm, cosy place it came from. In the same way, after we die our soul enters a new spiritual world.

## Prayer

Bahá'ís believe we should say prayers, read from the Word of God and meditate on it every day. This helps us to remember God's teachings. There are lots of Bahá'í prayers. This is a favourite prayer for many Bahá'í children:

> O God, *guide me, protect me, illumine the lamp of my heart and make me a brilliant star. Thou art the Mighty and Powerful.* - 'Abdu'l-Bahá

Adult Bahá'ís choose one out of three special daily prayers to say each day. This is one of them:

> *I bear witness,* O *my* God, *that Thou hast created me to know Thee and to worship Thee. I testify, at this moment, to my powerlessness and to Thy might, to my poverty and to Thy wealth. There is none other God but Thee, the Help in Peril, the Self-subsisting.* - Bahá'u'lláh

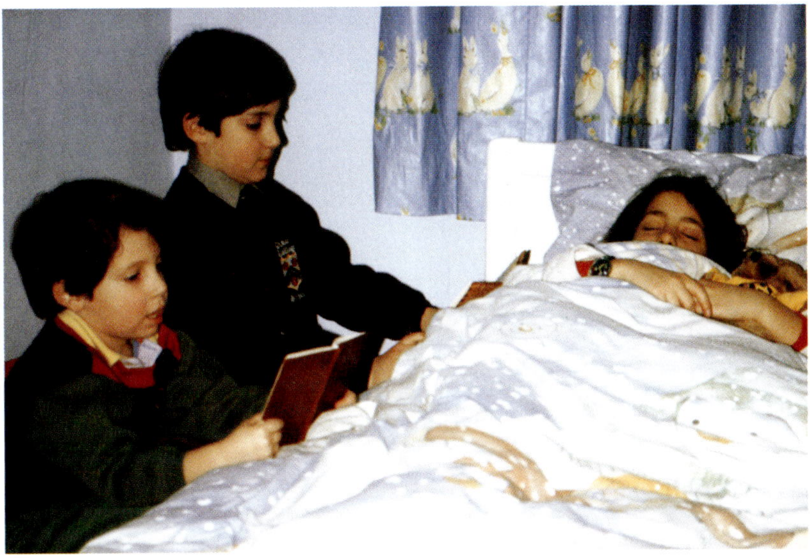

A prayer which many children learn is this healing prayer:

> *Thy name is my healing, O my God, and remembrance of Thee is my remedy. Nearness to Thee is my hope, and love for Thee is my companion. Thy mercy to me is my healing and my succour in both this world and the world to come. Thou, verily, art the All-Bountiful, the All-Knowing, the All-Wise.* - Bahá'u'lláh

This is a prayer for unity from 'Abdu'l-Bahá:

> *O Thou kind Lord. Unite all. Let the religions agree and make the nations one, so that they may see each other as one family and the whole earth as one home. May they all live together in perfect harmony.*

The History
of
The Bahá'í Faith

The old, walled city of 'Akká in Israel

# The Báb

The Báb was born in 1819 in Shíráz, Persia (Iran). In 1844 He announced that a great world teacher was coming. He said that many ideas of the time needed to change. But the king and the clergy hated the Báb's new ideas and had Him first imprisoned and then shot (in 1850). He is buried in this beautiful shrine. The shrine is in Haifa, in the Holy Land.

# Bahá'u'lláh

Bahá'u'lláh was born in Tehran, Persia, in 1817. He was a follower of the Báb. He had always been kind and generous to the people in His town, and was known as the 'Father of the Poor'. When the Báb was killed, many of His followers were tortured, killed or put into prison, just because they believed in Him. Bahá'u'lláh was put into chains in a terrible dungeon. Later, Bahá'u'lláh was sent away as a prisoner with all His family to Iraq, then to Turkey and then to 'Akká in the Holy Land.

The tall cloth hat (táj) worn by Bahá'u'lláh

In 1863, Bahá'u'lláh announced that He was the Promised One of all religions whom the Báb had talked about. He gave many new laws and ideas for our time. You will have read about some of them in this book. Bahá'ís are people who follow His teachings, and try to make the world a better place to live in.

‘Abdu’l-Bahá was the eldest son of Bahá’u’lláh. He was born on the very same night that the Báb first started teaching that a new religion was going to come. ‘Abdu’l-Bahá was only eight years old when he was sent far away from home with his Father and the rest of the family. They spent many years in prison.

When Bahá’u’lláh died, ‘Abdu’l-Bahá was the one who carried on teaching everyone to love people everywhere. ‘Abdu’l-Bahá was sixty-six years old when he was at last freed in 1908. He travelled to Egypt, Europe, Britain and North America, giving talks and helping people in need.

Community Life

# Bahá'í Children's Classes

Once a week Serene and Sahar go to a Bahá'í children's class. Bahá'í children are taught about all the religions of the world so that they can understand and love them all. Sometimes they put on plays for Bahá'í holy days, and take part in quiz games and sports days. They also learn prayers and sing songs and talk about the Bahá'í ideas you have read about.

# The Bahá'í Calendar

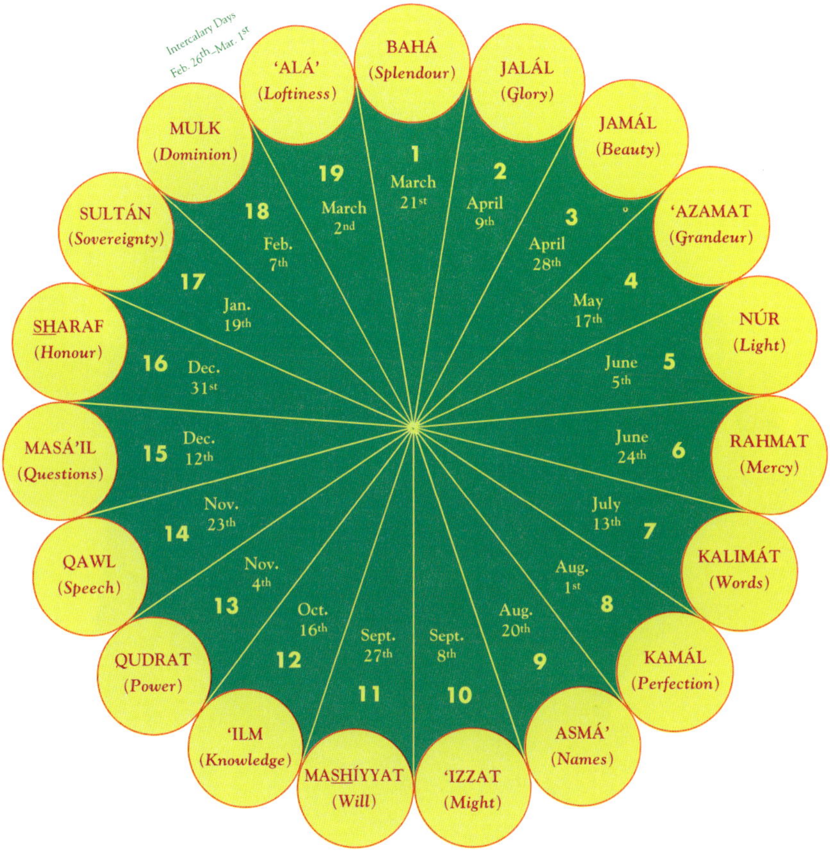


In the Bahá'í calendar there are nineteen months, each lasting nineteen days. The Bahá'í year starts on March 21st, the first day of the first month. The names of the months are words describing some of the qualities of God. You can see in the diagram above that one month is called 'knowledge' ('Ilm in Arabic). This helps Bahá'ís to think about the infinite knowledge of God.

# The Feast

In each town or village, the Bahá'ís come together every Bahá'í month for a meeting called the 'Feast'. The Feast is usually held in someone's home, but if the Bahá'í community is large they may have a Bahá'í Centre. Bahá'ís think that everybody should be proud of his or her own language, so prayers are often read or sung in several languages. After the

prayers and readings, everyone shares his or her ideas about community activities and plans, and even the children can join in. Then there is food and drink and everyone talks. It is important that everyone feels happy at the Feast - Serene and Sahar really enjoy it because they meet their Bahá'í friends.

# Bahá'í Holy Days

| | |
|---|---|
| ★ March 21 | **New Year's Day**<br>This is also the first day of Spring in the northern hemisphere. |
| ★ April 21<br>★ April 29<br>★ May 2 | **The Riḍván Festival**<br>These three days are very important to Bahá'ís because they are celebrated to remember the declaration by Bahá'u'lláh of His purpose. He made His announcement in a garden called Riḍván in 1863. |
| ★ May 23 | **The Declaration of the Báb**<br>The Báb made known His divine purpose on this day in 1844. |
| ★ May 29 | **The Ascension of Bahá'u'lláh**<br>On this day in 1892 Bahá'u'lláh passed away in the Holy Land. |

| | | |
|---|---|---|
| ★ | July 9 | **The Martyrdom of the Báb**<br>The Báb was killed in the city of Tabríz in Persia in 1850 on this day. |
| ★ | October 20 | **The Birth of the Báb**<br>The Báb was born on this day in 1819. |
| ★ | November 12 | **The Birth of Bahá'u'lláh**<br>Bahá'u'lláh was born on this day in 1817. Bahá'ís often celebrate this holy day with a big party for all their friends. |

Serene and Sahar, like other Bahá'í children, do not go to school on these special days. Bahá'ís celebrate their holy days in many different ways depending on their culture. They might all go on a big picnic, or meet to say prayers and share a meal. On New Year's Day, which is March 21st, Bahá'ís often have a special party. Serene and Sahar really look forward to their New Year.

# Bahá'í Weddings

Bahá'ís think that marriage is very important. It brings two families together, and a successful marriage gives children a happy home to grow up in. The Bahá'í wedding vows are very simple. The bride and groom each say one sentence:

*'We will all, verily, abide by the will of God.'*

The bride and groom choose their favourite prayers, readings and music because it is their special day. People in different countries have different customs for weddings, and Bahá'ís often marry people from other religions and cultures. The Bahá'í wedding allows people to keep their wedding customs.

The Bahá'í World
BAHA'I
BAHA'I

# Who is a Bahá'í?

'Abdu'l-Bahá was once asked, 'What is a Bahá'í?' and he replied that being a Bahá'í means 'to love all the world; to love humanity and try to serve it; to work for universal peace and universal brotherhood.'

There are Bahá'ís in nearly every country of the world, and they come from different religious, racial, national and social backgrounds.

# Bahá'í Assemblies

Delegates at a Bahá'í International Convention

Around the world, in every town or place, the Bahá'ís elect nine people to plan their activities. This group of nine people is called the Local Spiritual Assembly. There is also a National Spiritual Assembly for the whole country. There are 172 countries with National Spiritual Assemblies, and every five years their members choose nine people to serve on the Universal House of Justice for the whole world. They work to improve the world we live in. The photograph above is of the National Spiritual Assembly members in front of the building where the Universal House of Justice meets.

# Bahá'í Holy Places

Views of the Shrine of Bahá'u'lláh

Bahá'ís from all over the world go to Israel to visit the shrines where Bahá'u'lláh, the Báb and 'Abdu'l-Bahá are buried. This is called a pilgrimage. It is a very special time for a Bahá'í. Bahá'ís say prayers in the shrines, and visit the places where Bahá'u'lláh was imprisoned. This is one of the holy places Serene and Sahar hope to visit one day.

## Bahá'í Houses of Worship

House of Worship near Sydney, Australia

Inside the House of Worship near Sydney

House of Worship in Kampala, Uganda, Africa

Bahá'í House of Worship at Wilmette, near Chicago, USA

Bahá'í Houses of Worship have nine sides and nine doors, and are open to people of all religions. The nine sides show that there are many paths to God, and all

House of Worship near Frankfurt, in Germany

House of Worship in Panama, Central America

House of Worship near Apia, Western Samoa, South Pacific

House of Worship in New Delhi, India

religions lead to Him. Eventually they will have hospitals, schools and other buildings around them, and there will be Houses of Worship in every city.

## Social Projects

Bahá'í medical team

Ecology project in Italy

Because education for everybody is an important Bahá'í aim, many Bahá'ís in poor countries have started schools for the local children so that everyone

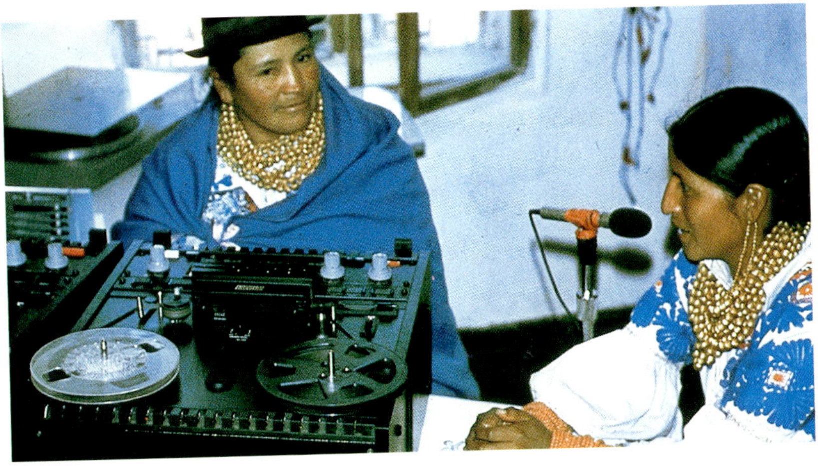

Bahá'í radio station in South America

Agricultural project in India

can learn to read and write. Very often Bahá'í centres are used for teaching better farming methods and for health education.

## Activities

1. Draw a garden with lots of different coloured flowers. Now draw a group of people with different coloured faces. See page 12.

2. What do you think you could do to help the poor people in the world? See page 15.

3. Look at page 16. Discuss how you think we can change things so that men and women are treated equally.

4. Look at page 19. First, write down any ways in which animals are treated wrongly. Now write down what you think are the proper ways to treat animals.

5. Look at page 20. Draw all the different symbols on this page and write the name of the religion they belong to next to each one.

6. Look at the list of great teachers on pages 22-23. Which ones have you heard of before?

7. Look at page 24, where it lists good ways of living. Which one do you think is the most difficult?

8. What do you think are the most important things that help our souls grow? See pages 24 and 26-27.

9. Read pages 10 to 27. There are a lot of ideas on these pages. Write down which ones you think are the most important for the world. Are there any others you can think of that would make the world a better place?

10. Why do Bahá'í children study all the world's religions? See pages 11, 20 and 34. Do you think this is a good idea?

11. Look at pages 38-39. Describe a religious festival in your religion, or write about how you would like to celebrate a special holy day.

12. Look at pages 46 and 47. Choose your favourite Bahá'í House of Worship and draw a picture of it. Write down what you like about it. If you prefer, you might like to draw your own design for a House of Worship. Remember, they all have nine sides.

13. Write about an idea for a project that would help people in the town where you live, or in another country. See pages 48 and 49.

# Topic Work

If you would like to do a topic on the Bahá'í Faith :

1. First describe how the religion started. Use pages 29, 30 and 31.

2. Second, write something about the great teachers, using pages 21-23 to start you off.

3. Third, write about some Bahá'í ideas, using pages 10-27.

4. Fourth, write about how Bahá'ís plan things, using page 44.

5. Lastly, add pictures of Houses of Worship or neatly write out one or two prayers. See pages 46 and 47 or pages 26 and 27).

The room in the house of the Báb in Shíráz where He declared His purpose in 1844

## Facts and Figures

There are about 5 million Bahá'ís in the world, from almost every race, ethnic group, religious denomination, and national and social background. From its beginnings in Iran in 1844, the Bahá'í Faith has grown so that now there are Bahá'í communities in almost every country in the world. According to the Encyclopaedia Britannica, the Bahá'í Faith is the most widespread religion after Christianity, with more than 120,000 centres. Bahá'í books have been translated into over 800 languages.

The Bahá'í Faith is not divided into sects. In every country with a large Bahá'í community, a National Spiritual Assembly is elected each year. There are 172 National Assemblies in the world today. In every local community where there are nine Bahá'ís or more, a Local Spiritual Assembly is elected. There are over 20,000 Local Assemblies around the world. Every five years the members of all the National Spiritual Assemblies from every corner of the globe travel to Haifa in Israel to elect the members of the international governing body of the Bahá'í community, the Universal House of Justice, and discuss the affairs of their Faith.

The Bahá'í Faith is recognized at international level, and works closely with the United Nations and some of its agencies, and the World Wide Fund for Nature.

International Archives Building at the Bahá'í World Centre in Haifa, Israel

## Glossary

**'Abdu'l-Bahá** This means the 'Servant of Bahá', a title given to the eldest son of Bahá'u'lláh.

**Báb, the** This means 'Gate', because the Báb was the gate leading to Bahá'u'lláh.

**Bahá'í** A follower of Bahá'u'lláh, someone who tries to follow His teachings.

**Bahá'í Centre** This is a meeting house or community centre where larger Bahá'í communities hold all their meetings like Feasts, holy days and assembly meetings. Smaller communities meet in the houses of Bahá'í families.

**Bahá'u'lláh** The founder of the Bahá'í Faith. Bahá'ís believe He was chosen by God. His name means 'The Glory of God'.

**Calendar** The Bahá'í calendar dates from 1844, when the Báb declared He was a Messenger of God. It has 19 months of 19 days each, plus some special days for visiting people and giving gifts. These special days make the year up to 365 days, or 366 in a leap year.

**Feast** This is the community meeting held every Bahá'í month (every 19 days), often referred to as the

Nineteen Day Feast. Bahá'ís from all over the community come together to say prayers, consult about community affairs and be together.

**Holy Land** The land of present-day Israel, and a place of pilgrimage of four world religions: Judaism, Christianity, Islam and the Bahá'í Faith.

**House of Worship** This is a Bahá'í temple, and people of all religions can worship there.

**Local Spiritual Assembly** Local Spiritual Assemblies look after the affairs of their local Bahá'í communities. They have nine members who are elected by the community and serve for one year.

**Messengers of God** These are the Prophets of the world religions, who bring God's message to us.

**National Spiritual Assembly** This is the national administrative body for Bahá'ís in a country. The nine members are elected once a year by delegates at a national convention.

**New Year** The Bahá'í New Year is called Naw-Rúz and is the first day of spring in the northern hemisphere and the first day of autumn in the South.

**Pilgrimage** For a Bahá'í, pilgrimage means visiting the

The headquarters of the Universal House of Justice, Haifa, Israel

holy shrines and places in the Holy Land. There are also holy places of pilgrimage in Iraq and Persia (Iran) where Bahá'u'lláh and the Báb lived.

**Prejudice** To be prejudiced usually means to think badly of someone because of their race, religion, nationality, sex or class. Sometimes people treat a person in a hurtful way because of their prejudice against him or her. Bahá'ís believe we should try to understand and love all people and not be prejudiced towards them.

**Promised One** Bahá'u'lláh said that He was the Promised One of all religions, and has come to fulfil their expectations.

**Riḍván** Riḍván means 'paradise' and is the name Bahá'u'lláh gave to the garden where He announced He was a Messenger from God.

**Universal House of Justice** The international governing body of the Bahá'í Faith. Its nine members are elected every five years.

**Word of God** The sacred writings of all the major world religions that contain the laws and teachings of their Prophet. Reading and thinking about (meditating on) the Word of God helps our souls develop.

Bahjí, near 'Akká, Israel, where Bahá'u'lláh died in 1892

# Index


'Abdu'l-Bahá 26-27, 32, 42, 45, 56
Abraham 22
Africa 46
'Akká 28, 30, 60
Animals 19, 50
Arabia 23
Australia 46
Avesta 22

Báb, the 23, 29, 30-31, 32, 38-39, 45, 53, 56, 59
Backbiting 24
Bahá'í Centre 36, 49, 56
Bahá'í class 34
Bahá'í community 33, 36, 44
Bahá'í ideas 10-27, 40, 42, 44, 51
Bahá'u'lláh 10, 11, 12, 23, 26-27, 30-31, 32, 38-39, 45, 56, 59, 60
Britain 32
Buddha 22
Buddhists 22

Calendar 35, 56
Central America 47
Children 11, 17, 26-27, 34, 37, 40, 48
Christians 23
Christianity 54, 57
Cleanliness 24
Confucius 23
Countries 10, 14-15, 40, 42, 44, 48, 54
Crops 9
Cruelty 19
Customs 13, 40

Death 24, 25
Differences 12, 13, 40, 43, 50
Disease 14

Earth 10, 19, 27
Education 17-18, 48-49

Egypt 22, 32
Equality 16, 50
Europe 32

Fairness 15, 24
Family 7, 9, 40
Farming 9, 49
Feast 36-37, 56-57
Fighting 13, 14
Flowers 12, 50
Food 15
Founders of religion 21-23
Friendliness 24

Generosity 24
Germany 47
God 12, 19, 20, 21-23, 24, 26-27, 35, 40, 46, 56-59
Government 14
Great Britain 32
Guru Nanak 23

Haifa 29, 54, 55, 58
Hard-working 24
Healing 27
Health 24, 49
Heart 26
Helping 14, 20, 24, 26, 32, 50, 51
Hindus 22
History 22, 28-32
Holy days 34, 38-39, 51, 56
Holy Land 29, 30, 38, 57
Holy places 45, 57-58
Honesty 24
Hospitals 47
Houses of Worship 46-47, 51, 52, 57
Human race 12, 42
Hunger 14, 15

India 22, 47, 49
Iraq 30, 59
Islam 57
Israel 28, 45, 54, 55, 57, 58, 60
Israelites 22
Italy 48

Jesus 23
Jews 22
Judaism 57

Kampala 46

Kindness 19, 24, 30
Knowledge 35
Krishna 22

Language 18, 36
Laws 22, 23, 31, 59
Local Spiritual Assemblies 44, 54, 57
Love 12, 20, 22, 32, 34, 42, 59

Marriage 40
Meetings 34, 36-37, 39
Messengers of God 21-23, 56, 57, 59
Money 15
Moses 22-23
Muhammad 23
Music 34, 36, 40

Nanak, Guru 23
National Spiritual Assemblies 44, 54, 57
New Delhi 47
New Year (Naw-Rúz) 38-39, 57
North America 32

Obedience 24
Oneness 10, 14

Pacific 47
Panama 47
Parents 9
Peace 10, 13, 20, 23, 42
Persia (Iran) 22-23, 29, 30, 39, 59
Pilgrimage 45, 57-59
Politeness 24
Pollution 14
Poverty 14, 15, 48, 50
Prayers 20, 24, 26-27, 34, 36-37, 39, 40, 45, 57
Prejudice 13, 59
Priests 23, 29
Prison 29, 30, 32
Promised One 23, 31, 59

Qur'án 23

Racial unity 12, 50
Radio Station 49
Reading 36, 37, 49
Readings 37, 40
Religions 8, 11, 20, 21-23, 27, 31, 34, 42, 46-47, 50-51, 57, 59

Respect 19, 20, 22

Samoa 47
Schools 17-18, 47, 48-49
Self-development 17, 20, 24, 59
Shíráz 29, 53
Shrines 29, 45, 59
Soul 24, 25, 50, 59
South America 49

Tabríz 39
Teachers 21-23, 29, 31, 50
Teachings 10, 20, 22-23, 26, 31, 54, 59
Tehran 30
Torah 22
Truthfulness 24
Turkey 30

Uganda 46
United States of America 46
Unity 13, 23, 27
United Nations 54
Universal House of Justice 44, 54, 59

Weddings 40
Western Samoa 47
Word of God 26, 59
Work 14, 20
World parliament 14
World language 18
World Wide Fund for Nature 54
Worship 26, 36-37, 46-47
Writing 49

Zoroaster 22
Zoroastrians 22